FABLE

A story of a Career spent gaining Wisdom

Our Story

This is the story of Jordan. A college student ready to take the working world by storm. Unfortunately, Jordan was neither the first, nor likely the last, to discover that what he had learned in school and in life to that point was a bit inadequate for navigating through the real world of FABLE. However, there was always help for those wise enough, or desperate enough, to seek it.

Beginning

Jordan was obviously excited when Franchised Amalgamated Blended Large Enterprise, which everyone referred to as FABLE, called with a job offer. School had been work but nothing he couldn't handle. Jordan held a variety of jobs through the four years of college, so beginning a career seemed like the "next step." An entry-level position at FABLE was perfect. Sure, Jordan was hoping one day for a job with clerical help, a high salary, wonderful benefits and a big corner office with a great view of the city. But first, it was going to be grunt work. Drudgery. A cubical in the center of the building on one of the lower floors.

"That's OK," thought Jordan, "I will move up quickly. I can do most anything for a few months."

Jordan approached the building on the first day, looked up at the imposing tower of a building, walked over the bridge spanning the reflecting pool, and thought, "I can't wait to show these folks a thing or two about how a business should really be run."

Yes, Jordan was all set. But what Jordan didn't know was that being all set, and being set to succeed, were two very different things. FABLE was a big place and, like all big places, had its own way of doing things. But on this bright day, his first day at FABLE, Jordan was blissfully unaware of what was true and what was false. Jordan, you see, was about to learn WISDOM.

A Bit Later

After working at FABLE for several months, Jordan realized that this work was somehow beneath him. Some entry-level people pushed a cart around all day, picking up things and moving those things to other places to be picked up again tomorrow. But Jordan was in a cubical. There was a magic box that displayed things from time to time. Sometimes those things seemed very important. Sometimes they didn't. In truth, Jordan had felt everything displayed on the screen was important at first. However, after several months the things on the screen stopped looking important, and Jordan noticed it was possible to do the job without paying much attention to the display at all. Jordan usually typed some variety of YES and pushed a button to clear the display or typed some variety of NO and pushed a button to clear the display. Occasionally, Jordan would see things on the display that made no sense.

"That's OK," Jordan thought, "As long as no one tells me anything different I can just keep doing what I do."

A few more months passed and Jordan realized that YES and NO were almost arbitrary. No one gave Jordan any feedback, so he eventually decided to spare himself the trouble of actually reading anything on the magic box and just respond with some version of YES or NO depending on who sent it or how Jordan felt at the moment. Jordan began to fill the day using the magic box to shop and catch up with friends from school. So seldom did anything displayed on the magic box mean much to Jordan that when one day something very important displayed, Jordan almost missed it.

Problem One

Jordan was in the middle of a lazy afternoon of looking at the magic box, writing some version of YES or NO, when a FABLE-wide communication went out. Typically, Jordan just glanced at the title, opened and quickly scanned the contents, then pushed the button that sent these sorts of useless messages to where ever they went when Jordan pushed the button. Jordan's finger was poised over the button and this stood out:

Due to a lack of productivity and profits at FABLE over the last several periods, the workforce will be RIGHTSIZED at the end of the month.

Jordan didn't know what "period" the message referred to. And he didn't know how FABLE measured "productivity" or "profits" because his job was to say some version of YES or NO and then use the magic box to keep up with friends or to shop for things. But one thing Jordan did know was that in a college class the professor had once used the term RIGHTSIZING and told the students that it was corporate code for some people losing their jobs. But because Jordan hadn't yet started his career, worrying about the whole rightsizing idea seemed kind of funny.

But now Jordan had a "real" job, and for reasons that were very obvious to him now, "rightsizing" spelled the end of Jordan's time at FABLE and the loss of easy access to a magic box to connect to friends and to shop. For the first time since beginning at FABLE, Jordan realized that things would have to change. And if things were going to change for the better, Jordan knew it was time to find someone who could explain what was going on and how to navigate this new dangerous situation.

Jordan asked a few of the folks who sat in their own cubicles every day with their own magic boxes what they thought of the message. Some of the cube dwellers had not even read the FABLE-wide message, while some simply looked back at their own magic box and kept writing some version of YES or NO and seemed content to ignore the impending doom that RIGHTSIZING represented. Not Jordan.

Suddenly Jordan saw that years of going to school could be taken away by the end of the month. No job meant no money. No money meant moving back home. Not eating out. No magic box. So, the next day during morning break, Jordan set out to find some help. One of the cube dwellers had said that there was a strange person down in the basement who always seemed to have an answer when he asked questions about things less important than RIGHTSIZING, but it was worth a try.

Navigating down to the lower levels of the FABLE tower was no easy task, but Jordan found a way. He made his way down to the boiler room where he saw a battered door. The nameplate on the door said INFORMATION. It seemed strange to have an information office way down here and not in the lobby, but maybe this information was different, he thought.

Jordan knocked on the door. No one answered right away and Jordan began to think he might just go back to the cubicle, but after walking all this way it seemed a waste not to try again. Jordan knocked again a bit louder, and he even put a little rhythm in the knock. This time the door opened, and sitting behind a battered desk was a young woman who looked about Jordan's age.

"Sorry to bother you," Jordan said, "But I was told that you might be able to help me by answering some questions about the all-FABLE communication that went out."

The young woman waved Jordan over to one of the two chairs in front of her desk.

"Have a seat, Jordan," she said. "I thought I might see you down here one day. What brings you by?"

"How do you know me? My name? Have we ever met?" Jordan asked.

"Well, that's a lot of questions, but not the question you came to ask. The answers are some form of YES to all three of the questions you asked and why don't you tell me specifically what brings you here today."

"Wait," Jordan said. "When did we meet?"

"It was a long time ago. You might not even remember. But, yes, I know you, Jordan. "So again, what specifically brings you here today?" she asked.

"Well, I want to know more about the all-FABLE communication we received. The one that talked about 'productivity' and 'profit', but mostly RIGHTSIZING," Jordan said.

She smiled and said, "Oh. Yes, I am familiar with that one. They mentioned the ol' RIGHTSIZING, didn't they? I had a professor say that one time, but she said it was a euphemism for people getting sacked."

"Mine said the same thing," Jordan said.

"I know," The woman said. "I think it is a standard speech they give sometimes in college business classes. But now the stakes have raised a bit, don't you think?" she asked.

Jordan replied, "Yes. Very much the stakes are up. I don't know the first thing about productivity, profit, or a whole lot of other things here at FABLE. I come to work. Do my job, then go home."

"I know. That makes you like most workers. You think if you are doing something and no one is telling you that you are doing it wrong, your paycheck hits the bank at the end of the month, so things must be fine. And you're right. They're fine. The problem is when RIGHTSIZING comes around your door, 'Fine' simply isn't good enough," the woman stated.

"Well, what do I do?! I don't want to be RIGHTSIZED! I only have until the end of the month to fix this or it might be me walking out the door with a box of my stuff in my hands. Can you tell me what to do?" Jordan asked.

The young woman looked at Jordan for a long time. Finally, she seemed to reach some decision and said, "I can tell you what to do. The problem is you won't do it. At least not for long. Just until the danger of RIGHTSIZING has passed."

Jordan was truly scared now. "So you won't help me?" he asked.

She cocked her head to the side and said, "I didn't say I can't help you. I said I wouldn't tell you what to do.

I'll help you, if you really want to be helped. But, it will be work. I'm not going to lie about that. You up for some work to save your job here at FABLE?"

"I am willing to do the work. I'll admit I haven't put much effort in beyond the minimum. But, no one said I needed to do better. Until now. Now it's real. How can you help?" Jordan asked.

The young woman said, "What I am going to tell you is pretty simple. It's a story really. It is probably one that you already know but just need reminding. But, if you promise to listen until the end and, more importantly, to see how this story is like your story here at FABLE, I think it might be a great help indeed. So, you in?"

Jordan swallowed hard and shook his head yes.

The young woman cupped her hand and put it to her ear. "I didn't hear you."

"Yes. I need the help and I am willing to listen and to think about what you say," Jordan said.

"Great! Actually saying the words to ask for help is important," said the young woman. "Let me tell you a story about Three Little Pigs and a Big Bad Wolf."

The Three Little Pigs

Once upon a time there were three little pigs. The pigs all lived at home, and as they got older, they wanted to move out on their own. So, each pig bought a piece of land and began to gather the materials to build his own house. The First Little Pig was not terribly hard-working and certainly wasn't interested in looking too far down the road. He was just interested in putting in his time, getting the house built in some form or fashion, and then getting on with the things he thought were more important--socializing with his friends, having a good time, and not working too hard. So, the First Little Pig built his house out of straw. It had walls, a roof, a door, and at least on the surface seemed like most other houses.

The Second Little Pig knew that he wanted a decent house to call home. So he gathered wood from the forest and built his house of sticks. He figured the day would come when things would change and he would be happy he had put the work in up front. As he built his house of sticks, he looked down the road and saw the First Little Pig with the completed straw house and asked himself if maybe he was overbuilding his own house. The First Little Pig was done with his work and had plenty of time to socialize and have fun. But, he thought, the day may come when I am glad a did a little extra work. He never even looked down the road at the Third Little Pig who was well known for working so hard it made the other pigs look bad.

The Third Little Pig KNEW that one day things would change. Maybe the weather. Maybe the circumstances. When that change happened the Third Little Pig wanted to be ready. So, she started gathering mud and made an oven. She baked many pallets of sturdy bricks. She took the time to design a plan for the house that would meet her needs now and in the future. She constructed the house with care and it took her a long time to do it. She looked down the road at the other two pigs and hoped that they would be OK when things changed. She didn't envy them the time they spent socializing and having fun because she knew that she was investing in her own future.

The other two Little Pigs stopped by and asked her to stop working so hard and go out with them to socialize, but she politely refused. She continued to work on her house and in the end had a sturdy, straight, well-built home that would last. When she was done she looked back on the hard work she had put in and the fun she had missed and decided the effort was worth it.

One day a Big Bad Wolf came to the neighborhood looking for bacon as Big Bad Wolves do. He spotted the houses of the Three Little Pigs. Coming to the front door of the straw house of the First Little Pig he knocked on the front door (which was actually an impressive feat to knock on a door made of straw). "Little pig, little pig, let me come in!"

And the First Little Pig said, "Not by the hair of my chinny chin chin."

The wolf relied, "If you don't open the door and let me in, I'll huff and I'll puff and I'll blow your house down!"

The First Little Pig said some version of NO so the wolf commenced to huff and puff and to blow the house down. As the straw started flying and it became apparent that the house was not structurally sound, the First Little Pig ran out the back and made straight for the house of the Second Little Pig.

The wolf arrived at the door of the Second Little Pig and knocked on the door (which was much easier with the wooden construction). "Little pig, little pig, let me come in!"

And the Second Little Pig said, "Not by the hair of my chinny chin chin."

The wolf relied, "If you don't open the door and let me in, I'll huff and I'll puff and I'll blow your house down!"

The Second Little Pig said some version of NO so the wolf commenced to huff and puff and to blow the house down. As the sticks started flying and it became apparent that the house was not structurally sound, both Little Pigs ran out the back and made straight for the house of the Third Little Pig.

The wolf arrived at the door of the Third Little Pig and knocked on the door (which was a lovely handmade six-panel variety). "Little pig, little pig, let me come in!"

And the Third Little Pig said, "Not by the hair of my chinny chin chin."

The wolf replied, "If you don't open the door and let me in, I'll huff and I'll puff and I'll blow your house down!"

The Third Little Pig said some version of NO so the wolf commenced to huff and puff and attempt to blow the house down. When no bricks started flying and it became apparent that the house was structurally sound, all the little pigs ran around and danced with joy. The wolf eventually went away as Big Bad Wolves eventually do.

The Third Little Pig said, "The danger is gone. Now you must go and fix your houses." The other two Little Pigs left, went back to their wrecked houses and started to rebuild. But they had not learned their lesson and rebuilt in the same manner with straw and sticks. When the Big Bad Wolf returned, as Big Bad Wolves typically do, this time he was successful in catching, and eating, the first two Little Pigs. This time there was no retreat for the first two Little Pigs to the brick house as the Third Little Pig was off on vacation to celebrate her recent promotion.

The End.

Aftermath I

"Wow," Jordan said. "I have heard the story before but killing the first two Little Pigs seems harsh."

"The world can be harsh, Jordan, but you know that. It's why you are down here talking to me," the young woman said.

Jordan said, "I understand the basics of the story, but I am thinking that there is more to it than I am seeing right now. You said you would help me. So, if you don't mind, would you walk me through the story and how it applies to me, FABLE, and RIGHTSIZING?"

"Certainly. I would be happy to do it," said the woman. "Although when I am done you will probably think it is super obvious. That is the thing about a good story. The right one not only makes the points clearly, but the person hearing it typically has a better chance of remembering those important points. For most of us it is more effective than if we hear 'Do this and don't do that.'"

Jordan smiled and replied, "I would be thrilled to have an OF COURSE moment about now. I am pretty desperate for answers to what I need to start, stop or change to avoid being RIGHTSIZED, so please, spell it out for me while I take a few notes in this notebook."

The young woman smiled back and said, "Really, it is pretty straightforward when you think about it. You have worked here for a while at FABLE and it seemed like everything was fine. It is because there were no BBW's, that's Big Bad Wolves, around. Now because productivity and profits are down, FABLE needs to RIGHTSIZE, which is just like the BBW knocking at your door. You, and the other workers here have all built your home, so to speak. Some of you have put in very little effort or time. You have done the minimum and focused your attention on socializing and shopping. Those are the houses made of straw because when the time comes to RIGHTSIZE, those are first to go because they are the easiest to find."

"The second group works a bit harder and a bit smarter. They have a sense of what is important and try to make sure that at least the most important things get done. No one is raving about their work, but there are fewer complaints. Sure, they are socializing and shopping some, but the at least the important stuff gets done. These are the houses of sticks. When the BBW knocks on their door they have some protection, but probably not enough in the long run. All this group needs are more focus and effort and they could really solidify their place here at FABLE.

The last group are the ones who treat other people they come into contact with as they would like to be treated. They don't just type some version of YES or NO, but instead really try to both meet the needs of other people and keep the goals of their department and FABLE in the forefront of their thinking. In addition, they have planned for their own future and use their efforts at their current position to help them further their careers. These are the houses of bricks. When the BBW comes to the door, they are aware but not worried. They know their previous work will likely guarantee them future employment unless true disaster strikes. This group is the last to get RIGHTSIZED, if ever."

Jordan was writing notes, but not every word the young lady said. In a way it was like being back in school. Jordan looked up slowly from the notebook with excitement.

"OF COURSE!" Jordan said. "I am sorry to say but I have been building my house of straw and now that the BBW, I mean RIGHTSIZING, is here I am in trouble. Wait! ...I'm in trouble here." And the excitement quickly faded from Jordan's face.

The young woman said, "You're right. You would be in trouble if the BBW was at your door right this instant. But, it's not. You have until the end of the month to build a better house for yourself! If you start today you can begin to build a better house that might get you through the first round of huffing and puffing. Just like the Second Little Pig. Maybe that is all it will take. This time."

She gave Jordan a serious look. "Most people only change when they have to. And you just realized you have to. But, to make a lasting change, to establish a new habit, if you will, takes at least 21 days. It looks like the end of the month is 24 days away. Perhaps if you really work on this plan every day, internalize the points from The Three Little Pigs, you can build a new house and ultimately a new career. I wish you great success! I hope for your sake, and for FABLE's, that it works out. I will be watching!"

Lessons I

After thanking the young woman for her help, Jordan returned to his cubicle.

"Only 24 days to make some important changes," Jordan thought.

After reviewing the notebook, Jordan took a little time and dedicated full pages as reminders of what the Young Lady had said. Jordan wrote:

There are three types of houses: Straw, Sticks, and Bricks. Only the last one survives so take the time to build that type of house for yourself.

Jordan's first months at FABLE were unfortunately spent building only a house of straw. Now the BBW was in the neighborhood and heading towards the door. It was time to get busy doing the things that should have been done before. Nothing could undo the choices he'd made before and the time he'd wasted. Those choices had been made before and could not be unmade.

If Jordan was to survive this round of RIGHTSIZING, there was no time to waste; he had to try at least to build a house of sticks. The Young Woman had said several things about the second group. Jordan used another page to write:

Always make sure the important things are done every day.

What Jordan had to do immediately was figure out what was important. It would be hard to make sure the important things were done every day if you had no idea what was important. Jordan began by looking at what information was readily available. Turning to the magic box, Jordan looked at the information that FABLE said about itself, its business and its goals. There was information about some of the bosses and how they had gotten into the company. After reviewing this information Jordan was able to determine with very little effort than one of the things that was important to the company at Jordan's level was that all communications were answered quickly and politely. In looking back at how he'd written some version of YES or some version of NO without much attention to why, Jordan realized he needed to pay closer attention to the individuals in the communications in order to be polite. That would allow Jordan to meet one of the primary goals of FABLE at his level. However, one of

FABLE's bigger goals was to provide a great experience for the customer with FABLE's products. So, Jordan wrote on another page:

Make sure all dealings with others focus on being polite and enhancing their experience with FABLE and its products.

If Jordan could keep these things in mind and stay focused on what was important, there was a chance the BBW of RIGHTSIZING would move past the door. This time.

At the end of the month the boss began to call people into his office. Some left happy. Some left sad. Finally, Jordan's time came. Entering the office almost didn't feel real. The years of college and the months at FABLE flew by in Jordan's mind.

The Boss said, "When the all-FABLE communication came out, I knew some of my least productive workers would be let go to meet my RIGHTSIZING goal. Frankly, you were on my initial list of people who would likely be let go. You were simply going through the motions. Writing some version of YES or some version of NO. But lately I have noticed not only a change in your productivity, but more importantly, a change in your attitude about your position here. The good news is you still have a job in the department. The bad news is you were the last person I kept. If another round of RIGHTSIZING comes along, you will be the first person I let go. Hear me when I say that your current efforts are better but won't be enough to save your job the next time around."

Jordan left the office neither happy nor sad. He was relieved to have a job but certain that the changes that began 24 days ago would need to continue. Jordan reflected on the things the Young Woman had said and knew that when the BBW came around next time, his house would be made of bricks.

Jordan continued to provide answers over the next 18 months that were still some version of YES or some version of NO, but there was a major difference. Now Jordan took the details of the situation and meshed those with the goal of both the department and FABLE. Jordan tried to find ways to say some version of YES more often, as long it was in line with department and FABLE policies. People began to write to the Boss and thank Jordan for the efforts made on their behalf. The next time a Boss summoned him into the office, Jordan learned HE was the new Boss of the department.

Over time Jordan was able to help many other employees by teaching them the importance of the lessons of the three houses, completing the important things, and treating people as they would want to be treated. Finally, of course, everyone needed to keep in mind the policies of the department and FABLE. The department became one of the most productive in FABLE, and Jordan was satisfied knowing the hard work was well worth the brick house he'd created.

Problem Two

After several years as the Boss of the department, there were some changes at FABLE. The longtime Leader of FABLE decided it was time to retire. After an "intergalactic search," the FABLE board hired a new Leader. Many were excited about the chance to have fresh ideas in the company at the top.

However, there were concerns in several departments when the new Leader actually began to make changes.

"Change is usually to be expected with new leadership," Jordan said at a team meeting shortly after the new Leader started in his position. "Let's give her a chance and see how things go."

Most of the people on Jordan's team were not directly impacted by the changes that the new Leader put in place. Initially more people were affected higher up the organization chart.

Jordan continued to build a house of bricks in the department. Customers were happy with his department's work, complaints were minimal and typically resolved before anyone outside the department was involved. Issues that went beyond Jordan were typically deemed unreasonable. All in all, Jordan was becoming a "Rock Star" in the FABLE world.

Things began to change in the Leader's second year at FABLE. The Leader began to make more and more decisions that affected people further down the organizational chart. As people began to take notice and speak up, the Leader began to find reasons to make those people, or their positions, disappear. Morale sank. However, people learned that speaking up was not the way to effect changes; it was the way to lose their jobs. So, a new culture took root at FABLE. No matter what happened or how things were changed, the employees all said, "Everything is great!"

But everything was not great. Not even close.

Jordan knew the changes being made were not leading toward long-term success. Productivity and profits were down in many of the individual departments which meant productivity and profits were down in FABLE as a whole. Meetings led to more meetings and there were charts and graphs displayed by different members at the top of the Organizational Chart explaining how "Everything is great!" But, it wasn't great.

Jordan noticed that presentations from the top people of the Organizational Chart didn't agree with the presentation before or the presentation after. Everything was said to paint a picture of FABLE that didn't match the reality of the employees' experience. From the outside everything appeared "Great!" But, to those inside FABLE, things were getting worse.

As people lost their jobs or their positions were RIGHTSIZED, others began to look for work elsewhere.

Often the ones who left were the best and brightest because other companies wanted them. When they left, often they were not replaced. Those remaining were asked to do their own work as well as the work of their departed colleagues and friends. This further drove down morale.

Jordan became increasingly concerned. It seemed that no one understood the seriousness of the situation. Jordan tried to talk discreetly with some of the bosses in other departments, but they said, "Everything is great!"

As weeks and months passed, Jordan became more frightened for FABLE's long-term viability. It seemed certain that another Big Bad Wolf was in the neighborhood. While Jordan's department was still solid, he knew it would not matter if the entire organization was in trouble. Jordan didn't know how a house of bricks could be built in just one successful department. However, thinking back to the last time a BBW had appeared, Jordan knew that it was time to get both good information and advice.

Jordan went back to the basement. And there by the boiler room found the door that had led him to the young woman in the past. But, there was no nameplate saying INFORMATION. The door was locked, and though Jordan knocked several times using a wide variety of rhythms, the door didn't open. Dejected, Jordan headed back to his office to consider his next move.

Because several of the elevators were not working and had not been fixed due to budget cuts, Jordan had to take the stairs. He was lost in thought before he realized he'd gone up one too many floors. Exiting the stairwell, Jordan looked across the hall and saw a door with the battered nameplate that said INFORMATION.

Hoping to speak with the Young Woman again, Jordan knocked on the door. After a brief pause, the door opened to reveal a Young Man about Jordan's age sitting behind a nice desk.

"I was wondering when I might see you."

Jordan was a little taken back.

"Do I know you? I was looking for the Young Woman who used to have that sign on her door."

The man smiled and said, "I think we have been through this before. Yes, you know me. We've met though you might not remember me. I am not exactly certain where the Young Women went, but I am here now. I have been hearing some rumblings of a BBW in the neighborhood. Is that what brings you here?"

"It is," said Jordan. "I don't know what to do. I have been working pretty hard to build my own house of bricks. Over time I have become the Boss of my department and have tried to help others build their own house of bricks which has put the department in a solid position. But with the new Leader, I don't think a brick house is going to be enough. I don't know what to do exactly. If you have any advice I would sure like to hear it."

"You are in a delicate situation," the Young Man said. "I don't know about advice, but your situation reminds me of a story. Perhaps you have heard of it. It is called 'The Emperor's New Clothes.'"

The Emperor's New Clothes

Once upon a time in a kingdom to the west a new Emperor was crowned. This emperor seemed to enjoy the job, socialized with the subjects, and always wore a smile. It wasn't long, however, before the Emperor began to believe his own press and thought he might, in fact, be the best Emperor in the world.

Maybe he was talented. Maybe he wasn't talented. But, there was little doubt that the Emperor was becoming more detached from the people of his kingdom with each passing moment. And those with a keen eye could see the Emperor was overmatched by the job. The economy was in decline, prices were up, and wages were down.

Some blamed the changes on the Emperor. Others thought he had come under the influence of advisors who had their own best interests at heart with little regard for the Emperor or the Empire.

One day a new designer of international acclaim arrived in town. She quickly arranged to meet with the

Emperor and informed him of her plans to create for him the most wonderful new suit of clothes ever made.

"It is only fitting," she said. "that a person of your position and talent have an outfit that shows your full majesty to the world. I will use only the finest materials and hand-stitch it myself– the finest designer in the world. The clothes will, of course, be expensive, but what is cost to one such as you?"

"It sounds lovely. I am the Emperor and undoubtedly have the talent for the job. I owe it to my people to appear in only the finest of clothing. Cost is no object because MY success is OUR success. The cost is irrelevant," said the Emperor.

"Well, the best part of this outfit will be its magical properties. Once it is complete and worn by you, it will only be visible to those who are worthy of seeing it! Those who are unworthy of their position, or fools, will be unable to see the outfit. In this way you will be able to weed out those people who should not be in positions of authority in the Empire, or perhaps even in the Empire at all!" said the designer.

And so began the construction of the magical outfit for the Emperor. In addition, the PR department was hard at work disseminating information Empire-wide about the magical properties of this particular outfit as well as the outstanding qualifications of this Emperor.

Months passed. Money flowed from the Empire's treasury to the designer. Finally, the outfit was ready.

The designer arrived at the castle and presented what appeared to the Emperor to be an empty hanger. Certainly a very nice hanger, but an empty one nonetheless. The Emperor was horrified. If he could not see the outfit it meant he was unqualified for his job or a fool. He decided immediately to pretend as if he could see the outfit. In time he assumed he would be able to see it like everyone else.

The designer helped the Emperor change into what was described as a multi-layered, silk-lined, fur-accented, jewel-encrusted ensemble. To the Emperor it just seemed drafty. Much of the Empire had gathered in the capital for a parade to view the new magical outfit. The Emperor was somewhat shaken at walking down the street when he could not see the clothes he was wearing but decided this was no time to turn back. So, the parade began.

A variety of bands, floats, and dignitaries were involved in the early portion of the parade with the Emperor walking with his honor guard at the end. As the parade commenced and the staff saw the Emperor, all had the same reaction.

"HE HAS NO CLOTHES!" they thought to themselves. For they remembered that these were magic clothes and those that could not see them were not qualified for their job or fools. So, they smiled, complimented the Emperor on the quality of the outfit, and put aside their own concerns. "I am sure, in time, I will be able to see the clothes" they all thought.

As the parade wound its way through the capitol, the citizens were all struck with the same thought, "HE HAS NO CLOTHES!" But like his advisors, they kept their smile on and their comments to themselves. "I am sure, in time, I will be able to see the clothes" they all thought.

Ultimately the Emperor passed a certain girl in the crowd. Now this girl was different. She was qualified for her job and she was nobody's fool. When she saw the Emperor, she saw he was there not in his new magic clothes, but in his birthday suit.

So, she said so.

A lot of motion and commotion followed. The Designer was jailed, the money confiscated. Well most of it. As these things go, sometimes all the money can't be recovered. Expenses and all.

The Emperor was embarrassed, exposed as a fraud, along with other less-flattering exposures, and removed from office. He was replaced by a much better Emperor, who was an intelligent lady from one of the noble houses. The girl who had been strong and courageous enough to speak the truth earned the new Emperor's trust and their friendship grew. But that is another story.

The End

Aftermath II

"Well that ended about how I remembered," said Jordan. "But I bet there are some things that I should be getting from the story that maybe I am missing. So, will you walk me back through it?"

"Certainly," the Young Man said. "Obviously the Emperor was a victim of his own pride and arrogance. You should remember that if you ever find yourself sitting in the Big Chair. You may find that is a different thing altogether than just being the Boss. The designer was able to take advantage of the fact that anyone who questioned the outfit was supposedly admitting their own incompetence or lack of intelligence. It was a smart pre-emptive move as it limited people's willingness to question what was going on."

"I have seen that in other companies where I have friends working," Jordan said. "People may have concerns about decisions being made but are afraid to speak up. If they are wrong, or if they are not believed, the price could be their job or even their career."

"That is absolutely true. Yet, the price of not speaking up is to watch a company, and many of its employees, suffer needlessly. Most people in the story, including the Emperor, had self-doubt. That doubt is so common psychologists have a name for it-- the Imposter Syndrome. This is when people doubt their own competence in a situation and feel they are just 'faking it.' It exists throughout the story and throughout many companies. People sometimes need help to learn to trust their own expertise," the Young Man said.

Jordan replied, "That is easier said than done. How can you improve your confidence in those situations?"

"One way is to make a prediction or plan a course of action and see how that would have turned out as events unfold. Obviously, if you have to make the call for real you might not get a practice run. But, often you can find a person to try your idea out on who can help work things out or validate what you were doing right," the Young Man said.

He continued, "One thing people often miss in this story is very specific to the girl who finally spoke up. People remember that she spoke up when others wouldn't, but they lose sight of what she said, and more importantly – what she DIDN'T say."

Jordan was puzzled. "What she didn't say?"

"Right," the Young Man said. "She said that the Emperor had no clothes. That was true and reflected what many others saw but didn't say. That alone was the important revelation that brought about change. What she didn't say was anything to do with how the Emperor looked without clothes. Nor did she laugh or try to make the situation even worse. Do you see the difference? The Emperor has no clothes is a statement of fact. Criticizing how he looked, laughing, or ridiculing him would either be mere opinion or simple cruelty. Neither is helpful and can overshadow the facts that are spoken."

As he closed his notebook, Jordan said, "You have given me a lot to think about. What the girl did seems easy, but my situation isn't."

The Young Man looked at him and gave him a warm smile. He said, "You are confusing easy and hard with simple and complex. What the girl did was simple. But nothing about it, or what you are facing, is easy. Take some time to think about it, and I am sure you will make the correct decision about how to proceed."

Lessons II

Jordan thanked the Young Man for his advice and headed back downstairs to his office. He opened the notebook and looked through the ideas he'd jotted down from the meeting. Several items jumped out at him as important, and Jordan decided to again summarize the key points on their own page. The first item was:

Good Leaders guard against falling victim to their own pride.

He knew this was something to guard against in the future. If the Leader trusts only himself or people who say everything is GREAT, it seems like he will shut himself off from a lot of really important information and advice. That doesn't mean everyone's opinion is of equal value, but a good leader must be willing to listen.

But to listen, someone has to be willing to speak up. That means employees who have knowledge the Leader needs have to feel safe and be courageous enough to share that information. This means:

Good employees speak up when the situation demands.

Knowing when to speak up and when to be silent is not always clear. This is where knowing that:

There is a difference
between
Easy/Hard &
Simple/Complex

This difference means doing the right thing can be simple to figure out, but complex to do. However, a good employee or leader will look for the right answers regardless of the complexity or ease of putting that right answer into place.

The final important lesson is about communication. Just like the girl in the story, it is important to state facts, not opinions. Those facts needed to be said without turning the statement into an opinion or being cruel. Jordan wrote:

Speak up when it is called for with the FACTS without cruelty or needless embarrassment.

Jordan looked over the notes and thought about what the right course of action. It was an important decision, so Jordan invested several days of thought. Ultimately, he decided, speaking up was clearly the right call. There was no denying that it was also a hard thing to do. It was possible that Jordan's job, and perhaps career, would hang in the balance. However, Jordan decided that doing the right thing was always the option he'd choose moving forward.

There was a staff meeting held a week later. All department heads and leadership at FABLE were present. The Leader was running the meeting. After a presentation about how GREAT everything was at FABLE, many in the audience were looking at their laps. When the time for questions came, the first few people who spoke up began with some form of FLATTERY then asked softball questions. The Leader answered and seemed very pleased.

Jordan decided it was time.

"I am confused. The information we have received over the last year indicates that both productivity and profits are down. Good people are losing their jobs. Are you saying that this is our new normal or is this part of a general turnaround in our fortunes at FABLE?"

The room got very quiet. The Leader got very red in the face. The leader was used to some form of FLATTERY rather than truth when people spoke to him. When confronted with the hard facts, the Leader was not prepared to answer.

"Everything is GREAT at FABLE! Clearly you don't understand! I am not certain you are in a position to be questioning me," the Leader said.

The meeting quickly ended. As the room emptied many people approached and said some form of THANK YOU because Jordan had said what they all knew to be true.

Things were not smooth for a while. The Leader planned on firing Jordan, but Jordan's record as a Boss as well as his simple, factual question didn't give adequate grounds for dismissal. Certainly, some leaders could have fired Jordan anyway, and may have done so. However, word soon spread to the Board of a Boss who had asked a factual question of the Leader that he could not answer. The Board realized they had hired a person who had only his own best interest in mind and not that of FABLE. A buyout ensued, and a new Leader was chosen.

No, the new Leader was not Jordan. Jordan was unqualified to be the Leader of an organization as large and complex as FABLE. However, the Board took notice of Jordan and his willingness to appropriately speak up when the situation merited. This led to other opportunities for Jordan which led to new situations and questions.

Problem Three

Years passed and Jordan continued in the role of Boss. While he enjoyed being successful in the current role, the position was not really a great challenge any longer. Certainly, there were problems to be solved, crises to confront, and personnel issues to manage, but those involved the application of lessons already learned.

Jordan had enjoyed the current position of Boss for a long while. Every morning he looked in the mirror and smiled at the prospect of going to work. But frankly, the smile was beginning to fade. He found the job less challenging than he once had, and with this lack of challenge was the inevitable lack of growth.

Boredom was a big threat to the Brick House that Jordan had built in the department. It could easily lead to lack of attention to detail and poor customer service which would doubtlessly lead to a drop in productivity and profit in the department as well. Jordan decided it was time to consider other opportunities.

Using the magic box, Jordan began looking for new jobs and found two potential positions in FABLE and one outside of FABLE. Jordan was both excited and a bit nervous about switching jobs. However, the prospect of stagnating in the current position of Boss of the current department was something that would be fair to neither Jordan nor FABLE.

The three new positions all carried their own challenges and rewards. All of the positions were a step up from the current role of Boss. However, leaving a place where Jordan had complete command of all parts of the job and had successfully faced a version of EVERY PROBLEM and moving to a new job where all of the answers would not perhaps be so readily apparent was a least a bit intimidating.

As the deadlines for the applications for the three positions loomed, Jordan was still unsure for which of the three to apply. Each had their own pluses and minuses.

Having made a T-chart and slept on the problem for several nights, Jordan was no closer to a decision than when the postings first appeared on the magic box. Seeing no answer in sight, Jordan climbed the stairs and headed for the room marked INFORMATION.

As had happened last time, the door was there, but the plate on the door was not. Jordan knocked, but received no answer.

"Hold on a moment," Jordan said. "I remember this! I guess I need to look around a bit more for the advice I need."

Sure enough, one floor up and a down the hall a bit, Jordan spotted the familiar name plate on the door-- INFORMATION. Smiling, Jordan rapped on the door and after a slight pause it opened to reveal a Woman about Jordan's age sitting at a much nicer desk than before. Jordan took in the room at a glance and noticed multiple plaques and awards as well as pictures of the Woman shaking hands with important people that Jordan knew.

"Jordan!" said the woman. "I am so glad you stopped by. I was beginning to wonder if I would see you anytime soon. And now, here you are!"

The woman didn't look entirely familiar to Jordan, but by this point Jordan was just going to roll with it. The Woman's enthusiasm was infectious and reminded Jordan of the first few weeks as the Boss. That feeling seemed to have slipped away when Jordan didn't notice. But, Jordan knew that it was past time to get that feeling back.

"I am in a bit of a quandary," Jordan began. "I think I am good at my position as Boss, but the excitement just isn't there every day. I have begun to look around for a new challenge and have found three that are interesting for different reasons. Now I am not certain which one, or ones, I should apply for. I know it is time to make a change, but I am bit unsure of which way to go. I was hoping you might have some time to give me some advice."

The Woman smiled.

"I would love to help! Taking a moment to try to mentor someone who needs, but more importantly wants, the help is going to make this a great day for me. Do me a favor. Don't tell me about the jobs. I don't need to know, and I think it would be better if I didn't know. You see, I don't want to give you advice based on what I think might be best from my point of view. That would get in the way of what might actually BE best in your situation."

Jordan frowned. "But, I want your input. I would like your opinion."

"I am flattered," the woman replied. "But, I would rather give you some good information and from that you are more than capable of forming your own opinion and coming up with the right answer. So, have you ever heard the story of Goldilocks & The Three Bears?"

Goldilocks & The Three Bears

Once upon a time there was a young girl named Goldilocks who lived near a forest. She would frequently walk in the forest, but one day she became distracted, then lost. She wandered deeper into the wood than she had ever done before. As she walked along she became hungry, but there was no food to eat.

Suddenly, over the top of the trees she saw smoke. She headed towards it and came upon a sturdy cabin in the woods. The smoke rising from the chimney made her hopeful that she would be able to find some food. Goldilocks knocked on the door, but no one answered. She knocked again with the same result. Overcome with hunger, she tried the doorknob and found the door was unlocked. Goldilocks went in.

Had she looked around, she may have noticed a nice family portrait of three bears on the wall. Bu,t Goldilocks only had eyes for the three bowls sitting at the dinner table. Walking near she saw that each contained porridge.

Goldilocks sat down at the head of the table, picked up the spoon beside the bowl, and took a big mouthful of porridge. Instantly she regretted it. The scalding porridge burned her tongue and the roof of her mouth in the way that only steaming hot porridge can. Goldilocks spit some, swallowed some and cried some. Eventually, she was able to quit crying and set the spoon down.

Goldilocks went to the other end of the table and sat down, still hungry but much more cautious. She took the spoon beside the bowl, scooped up some porridge, slowly brought it to her mouth, blew on it furiously and took a bite. No burning, but the porridge was cold and wholly unsatisfying in the way that only cold porridge can be. She avoided spitting it out, and frankly the cool porridge did wonders for her burnt mouth. Still, Goldilocks, as hungry as she was, decided to try the third option.

Moving to the chair in the middle, she picked up the spoon by the bowl, scooped up a bite of porridge, blew on it, and cautiously took a bite. It was Perfect! A little hotter than warm with brown sugar, cinnamon, and a splash of milk. Goldilocks dug in and quickly finished the entire bowl.

Pushing away from the table, stomach full of wonderfully perfect porridge, Goldilocks realized that she was at the end of a very long day. Across the room she spotted a big bed and thought it would be wonderful to lay down. She went to the bed, jumped up and landed flat on top. She may as well have landed flat on the floor as the bed was way past ultra-firm mattress range.

Goldilocks crawled off the bed and went to the next one. She jumped a bit more cautiously into the next bed and felt like she was being swallowed by the bed as it was so soft she sank about a foot into the mattress. While she was uninjured, she was not willing to try to sleep in a bed that might smother her.

Goldilocks managed to get out of the bed and went to the third bed. She cautiously crawled in. It was Perfect! The bed had just the right amount of support and a wonderful pillow designed for a side sleeper like Goldilocks. She pulled up the down comforter and fed, comfortable, and tired, fell fast asleep.

While she was sleeping the Three Bears came home. They went to the table and before the could sit down to eat they noticed that someone else had been there. Papa Bear said, "Someone has been eating my porridge! And they have spit stuff all over the bowl and the table cloth, and that's just wrong."

Mama Bear said, "Someone has been eating my porridge, too. There is a scoop out of the middle and some is still stuck on the spoon. Not good."

Baby Bear said, "You guys got off lucky as my porridge is all gone! I told you, brown sugar and cinnamon with a dash of milk was the way to go."

"Well I've lost my appetite," said Papa Bear.

"Me, too," said Mama Bear. "I am just going to go to bed."

"Good idea," said Papa Bear.

"Well, I am still hungry," said Baby Bear.

"Then have a peanut butter and jelly sandwich or go to bed. Your choice," said Papa Bear and Mama bear in unison.

Baby Bear looked sad, but said, "Fine. I'll just go to bed."

They turned off the lights and headed to their rooms.

Papa Bear said, "Someone has been in my bed! The blankets are messed up and my pillow has been moved. That's just wrong."

Mama Bear said, "Someone has been in my bed, too. The sheets have shoe marks and it looks like someone has been wrestling in there. Not good."

Baby Bear said, "You guys got off lucky again because the person is still IN my bed. I told you the adjustable bed was the way to go."

"Well I think we should wake her up," said Papa Bear.

"Me, too," said Mama Bear

"Well, I think we should just let her sleep until the morning. I'm going to go make that PB&J sandwich after all. I can just sleep on the couch tonight," said Baby Bear.

So, they let Goldilocks sleep. In the morning, after an awkward round of introductions, the family escorted her to her part of the forest and from there Goldilocks returned home safely.

The End

Aftermath III

Jordan said, "Well, that story had a better ending than one someone told me a while ago about Three Little Pigs. So, Goldilocks makes it out alive."

"True enough," said the Woman. "There is a happier ending here. But, I think the same is true of what you should take away from the story. Your future looks bright to me."

"Thanks. However, I am confused about how to move forward. The options I have all seem like they would be great. So, it makes it difficult to choose," said Jordan.

"Perhaps at first glance all the options look equally great. But, maybe if you look closer you will discover that there are differences. When Goldilocks was lost in the forest, the house looked like her salvation. And it was. Just like you, she was looking for something and she found something. At least at the outset, this represented a 'can't lose' proposition," said the Woman.

Jordan thought for a moment about his own search for a way out of his current situation. "I certainly see the connection. Bu,t did Goldilocks really have three good options?"

"Well she had three OPTIONS. But, that is very different than three good OPTIONS," said the Woman. "Think back. When Goldilocks entered the house, she was lost in the woods. Now at least she had a roof over her head. That is probably an improvement, depending on what happens inside the house."

"What does that mean?" asked Jordan.

"Think about it for a second," said the Woman. "What if it was the witch's house from Hansel and Gretel? Good chance she went from the outdoors into the oven. Right?"

"Oh, just because you made it inside doesn't mean you are safe," said Jordan.

"Exactly!" said the Woman. "Let's take a closer look. Once inside she found she was hungry and had three choices. The first choice seemed great because it was the first choice. Yet she burned herself. The second choice was safer than the first, but not very satisfying. The third choice was PERFECT. She ended up eating all of that porridge and was very satisfied that she did."

"So sometimes it is better to pass on the first few options?" asked Jordan.

"Sometimes, yes. But, the order is not what is important. It is the suitability. She sat down at one chair and it was wrong. What if she had sat down at Baby Bear's chair first? She would have had a great meal, but never would have known what else was out there," said the Woman.

She continued. "Let's move on to the sleeping arrangements. Again, the first one almost hurt her when she blindly jumped in because it was so hard. The second one almost smothered her because it was too soft. Only the last option was PERFECT. That is what you are looking for. The PERFECT option. If you can find it."

"'If you can find it' doesn't sound promising," said Jordan.

The Woman smiled. "Oh, it is very promising, I assure you. The secret is to look at the signs that are there to see. Steam coming off the first bowl, none on the second for example. Use the information available to investigate and make a wise choice. Don't just dive in at the first option you see. If you put in some time to investigate you will likely see what job is closest to PERFECT. Now, don't be confused. Sometimes you have to apply for the job as part of your investigation. Then through the hiring process you investigate the company and the position and make a wise decision."

Jordan sighed and closed the notebook he was writing in. "It looks like I have some thinking and investigating to do over the next several weeks."

The Woman smiled again. "Now you get it! You are faced with a big decision, but not one that requires an immediate answer. You are smart. You are successful. Use that to evaluate your three choices and I am sure it will turn out PERFECT."

Lessons III

Jordan headed back to the office to review what had been discussed. In looking through the notes, Jordan realized one important thing to remember. When someone's in a situation she wants out of, almost any solution looks better than it might be in reality. In thinking about the fact that Goldilocks entered a house in the woods with no idea of who lived there, it made Jordan pause.

"Perhaps I have also just decided to run into any house available?" Jordan asked. Jordan decided a reminder was in order and wrote this on its own page:

When seeking a safe place to go, any place can look safe at first glance.

However, learning from the Goldilocks story that it was important to investigate the options, don't just jump in as it was very possible to get hurt or trapped. Jordan realized that only by looking at the information available and taking some time to analyze the information can a person make a wise decision. Jordan wrote:

Take time to observe and analyze the available information before making an important decision.

In reviewing the story of the interaction of Goldilocks with the Three Bears, it seemed that one of the most important lessons to learn was that while Goldilocks had three options, she really only had one good option. The one she had deemed PERFECT. Now, perfection might be a bit of a stretch, but realizing one option was clearly the best was not a stretch at all. One of the options in this case was not just wrong it proved injurious. Another was easy. In fact, it was distastefully easy. Jordan wrote:

If possible, eliminate potential options that are obviously harmful or obviously unsatisfying.

"Obviously in a real emergency, or if there was only one option available, you might need to take an option that was less than ideal," Jordan thought. "But, it would at least be better if people went in with their eyes open."

Jordan thought there seemed to be one more lesson here to note. The Baby Bear choice was the PERFECT choice, when it was available. It was the one that was satisfying without being too much or too little. In the end the Baby Bear choice led to new friends, increased satisfaction, and greater safety. Jordan wrote one last note:

The Perfect Choice is the one that enhances friendships, satisfaction, and safety.

With these new ideas in mind, Jordan decided to review the potential job openings. In the end, it didn't seem that enough information was yet available to eliminate or embrace two of them. The third choice seemed to be a Mama Bear Choice within FABLE. Jordan decided that while the position would be different, it would also be too easy and would quickly lead to boredom doing a job that Jordan really didn't want to do. That left the other two options. One inside and one outside of FABLE.

Jordan applied for both and was granted interviews. After the second interview with the outside company, Jordan realized that the position had little job security and few prospects for success. After reviewing the information gathered from the interviews, Jordan sent a politely worded letter withdrawing from consideration.

The FABLE position was exciting. The area interested him and was different than his current job.

Jordan spent many hours preparing for the third and final interview.

The hiring committee saw in Jordan exactly what they were looking for. Jordan thought the position was PERFECT. When the Human Resources person called, Jordan was able to quickly say some version of YES.

This started a new chapter in Jordan's career. One that led through multiple successes, and a few failures. For what good story doesn't have a failure or two?

Problem Four

Jordan enjoyed the new position. That position led to another within FABLE. And so on. And so on until many years had passed.

Jordan had now been the Leader of FABLE for several years. The Board had remembered the young Boss who was willing to speak up when the Emperor had no clothes. They had watched while Jordan pursued a position that was a challenge successfully met. Ultimately, they saw that Jordan was the person to lead FABLE through the next phase of corporate life.

Unfortunately Jordan, like all leaders, was not always successful. After experiencing a time of declining revenue, Jordan saw an opportunity to grow FABLE and move into some new areas of business, so he endorsed a merger deal with a rival company. While Jordan had helped foster a culture of mutual support and positive growth within FABLE, the potential merger company did not share this same philosophy. New Industrial Growth Harvesting

Team or NIGHT was definitely a growing company with a dynamic and persuasive leader. However, the employees shared a ruthless mindset that, while profitable, was not always pleasant. Employees came and went, but only the strong and competitive were really successful.

So why didn't Jordan see the truth of the cultural difference? Because the Company was called NIGHT and the people weren't wearing shirts saying, "I'm Cutthroat." The corporate methodology was always somewhat of a mystery to people outside the upper reaches of the company.

Jordan was fooled. The Board was fooled. Most of the people in the world were fooled. While NIGHT was not making the list of MOST ADMIRED companies, they often made the list of MOST PROFITABLE companies. This we know is totally different.

Jordan had done well in negotiating the merger. There was a provision in the legalese of the merger agreement that if FABLE was able to increase profitability 19% above the previous year's mark, then FABLE could call off the merger if they chose. But, why would they?

This question was answered when one of Jordan's VPs overheard two VP's from NIGHT at a random coffeehouse talking about the plan to fire Jordan along with 40% of the FABLE employees shortly after the merger became final in just over six months.

When the VP brought the information to Jordan the truth set in. "We are in trouble," Jordan said. "I am afraid I have led us into a problem that will cost many of us our Jobs and Pensions, and me most of my self-respect. Saying I'm sorry doesn't even begin to cover the damage that is about to be done."

Charlie, the VP who had brought the news said, "Not gonna lie, Boss. It looks grim. But, we have faith in you as the Leader. You'll figure it out, I'm sure."

The meeting broke up, and word of the meeting spread throughout FABLE as bad news always does.

But, Jordan wasn't so sure there was a way out. There were possibilities, but time was not on FABLE's side. As one of the people who had put together the merger agreement, Jordan knew the provision to raise the profits 19% was a possible escape clause. However, raising annual profits by 19% in only half a year seemed out of reach.

Jordan spent the next several days trying to figure out FABLE's exact financial position and brainstormed some ideas with the Leadership Team about ways to cut costs and raise revenues. Their efforts, if fully-implemented, would render a massive 4% increase to profitability in only ten days. However, it came at the cost of a 15% staff reduction. If they went through with the plan, Jordan didn't think that made FABLE much better than the folks over at NIGHT.

Jordan sat in the Big Chair behind the Big Desk in the Big Office at the top of the Big Tower.

"I don't recall ever feeling quite this alone surrounded by this many people."

Jordan decided to go out, walk around and just talk to some of the employees. The walk covered most of the departments and many of the floors of the building. Jordan did all that was possible to encourage the employees of FABLE. In the end, he hoped they felt better about the prospects for the merger. However, Jordan was pretty certain that things would not end well.

While heading back after dark through one last hallway a floor down from the big office, Jordan spotted the old INFORMATION plate on a door. Realization dawned.

"I have been trying to figure everything out mostly on my own with a bit of help from my Leadership Team. I think it is time to ask around and listen instead." Jordan smiled and knocked on the door.

The door swung open to reveal a Middle-Aged Man behind a large desk.

"Jordan. Good to see you. But, I have to be honest. You've looked better."

"Thanks. I've felt better," Jordan replied.

"What brings you down here out of the Big Chair?" the man asked. "I thought the Leadership Team was hard at work on a plan to save FABLE?"

"We've tried, but we can't discover a way to void the Merger Agreement with NIGHT. It is my fault we are in this mess, and I need to find a way out," Jordan said forcefully.

"And I guess you haven't singlehandedly figured it out? No surprise. No offense, but that is a Big task no matter how Big the office, Big the chair, or Big the person. See, you just said some things that aren't true. Most importantly, it is not your FAULT. Plenty of people, including the Board, signed off on this decision. Bu,t as the Leader it is your RESPONSIBILITY. The chances of you figuring it out by yourself, carrying out the plan by yourself, and snatching victory from the jaws of defeat by yourself are pretty slim," the Middle-Aged Man said shaking his head.

"I am open to suggestions," Jordan said.

The Middle-Aged Man paused for a bit, then said, "You always were. That is one of your best qualities. I hope now that you are at the top of the org chart the same is still true. So, have you heard the story of Rumpelstiltskin?"

Rumpelstiltskin

One upon a time there was a miller who lived in a beautiful kingdom. The miller was overheard to say that his daughter was the best thread spinner in the world. A spinner so skilled she could spin straw into gold.

Well, it didn't take long for word to reach the greedy king of the beautiful kingdom. He called the miller's daughter to the castle and unceremoniously threw her in a room with two bales of straw and a spinning wheel. "Spin this straw into gold by tomorrow morning or I will have you put to death for lying to the king!" So saying, the king left and locked the door behind him.

The woman was stunned and afraid. "How did this happen?" She asked. "I didn't make that claim! It was my Dad. Doesn't anyone understand parental hyperbole?"

"I do," said a voice from the corner. Turning around she saw a strange man with a strange look on his face. "I understand hyperbole, and I also understand the way of deals. What deal can you make for me to spare you from death in the morning if I spin this straw into gold?"

"I will give you this necklace I am wearing. It was my mother's before she died. I swore I would never part with it. But, if you can do as you say I will give it to you," the woman said.

"Done." said the man. "I will take the necklace in the morning when this straw is all gold."

The next morning the king returned and to his amazement the straw was gone and in its place were spools of the finest gold thread ever seen in the kingdom. "Well done! I always knew you could do it! Now that I know you are the real deal I have something to show you."

The king led the woman to another room filled with ten bales of straw. "Your wildest dreams are about to come true! Turn this into gold by morning and I will marry you and make you queen. Fail, and it will be your death. Exciting. I know."

But, the woman was not excited. As she was locked into the new room she knew that her death awaited her in the morning. "I can't make this straw into gold thread by myself. I am not terribly happy about being married to a man who just threatened to kill me, but one thing at a time."

"Yes, one thing at a time," said the voice behind her.

Again, when she turned around she saw the strange man. "I have nothing left to give you, sir. So even if you help me it would have to be for free," the woman said.

Without saying a word, the man went to the spinning wheel and began to spin the straw into gold. As morning approached the man finished the spinning.

"Remember the Golden Rule! He who has the gold makes the rules. I will take your firstborn child as payment for my services when he or she arrives." And then he vanished.

The woman was still stunned thinking about implied contracts, bad faith negotiating, and what had just transpired, when the king entered.

"Splendid!" he said as he surveyed the gold thread. "Send out the word that there will shortly be a royal wedding."

And there was. It turned out that the king was greedy, and had threatened to kill her because of it, but she was not always unhappy. After a few years she gave birth to a son.

That night the now Queen again heard the voice of the man behind her.

"I am here for the child," he said.

"Wait! I could not possibly part with him as he has just been born. I did not agree to this deal," the Queen said

"Nor did you decline it," the man said.

The Queen relied, "True. But, is there another deal we could make?"

"I am a reasonable man," the man replied, although he really wasn't. "Tell you what. If you can tell me my name in three months time with only three guesses at the end of each month, I will let you keep the child and I will go on my way. Otherwise our agreement for me to take the child stands and WILL be enforced. Do you agree?"

"I do," said the queen. The man disappeared and the queen despaired. Fortunately, she had a baby name book among the baby shower gifts.

She poured over the book and at the end of the month tried the three least common names she found. The strange man just laughed at her. "Not even close," he said. You better put more effort in. So, she did. She consulted her royal advisors about names and made many lists and gave it much thought and consideration.

At the end of the second month she tried three very common names because the advisors had thought straightforward was the best option. "Again. Not even close. You will have to be smarter than that or the child is mine at the end of the month!" the man said while he laughed at her.

So, she thought about it more and decided that her advisors and the strange man were both right. She decided to be even more straightforward and smarter at the same time. She told the king about what had happened and decided to go to the people and ask for help.

The day before the man was to reappear, one of the citizens arrived at the castle to tell her the story of seeing a strange man singing to himself.

"He said, 'The child will be mine! It will be fine! I will win or I'm not Rumpelstiltskin!'"

While that was certainly no name she had heard before, she thought if her own two best guesses didn't work she would try that name out of desperation. The next day the man appeared. The Queen tried first one name, then another. The man just laughed. "It is as if you are not even trying! The child will be mine!"

It finally clicked in the Queen's head. A smile spread over her face. She said, "No the child is mine! WE will be fine. I shall win. For is your name not Rumpelstiltskin?"

A looked of anger spread over his face. He sputtered in rage. But, a deal was a deal. The Queen said, "Guards, escort this man from our castle." He left and the Queen was happily left with her child.

The End

Aftermath IV

"Wow!" said Jordan. "I do like a happy ending. But, it seemed like a mess that could have been avoided if people would have spoken up earlier."

"Sure," said the Middle-Aged Man. "Looking back, it is usually easier to see the wrong turn you made. Or where the price you now face is a lot higher than speaking up when the time was right. But, life doesn't seem to work that way all the time."

"If ever," said Jordan. "So, let's walk through this. I have some notes, and I knew the basic story, but I want to hear your take on things."

"Sure. Let's start at the beginning. The future queen got in trouble when she let someone else speak about her in a way that she knew to not be true. It was flattering. It was her Dad. But so what? Look at the price she had to pay. The comments couldn't have been true. Straw into gold! Seriously?" The Middle-Aged Man said.

"That is true," said Jordan. "It is easy to hear flattering things and chalk them up to Hyperbole. I am sure she never imagined the price."

The Middle-Aged Man smiled. "I am sure she didn't. But, the price was no less real. Let's move on. She found herself in a mess and didn't have the tools or the talent to extract herself from the mess on her own. When we find ourselves in those situations it is easy for others with low character to take advantage of our problems. Enter Rumpelstiltskin. The first price, her mother's ring, was high but manageable. She convinced herself she had no other option. Maybe she did. Maybe she didn't. Either way, she took the deal. Remember, even though she got out with her child in the end, he left with her mother's ring. That wasn't coming back. It was just gone. What happened next?"

"It didn't really get her out of the mess she was in. The King just wanted more," Jordan replied.

"Exactly!" the Middle-Aged Man said. "The king wanted more, but she thought she had nothing more to trade. Rumpelstiltskin showed her that to people with bad intentions, there is always more to take. Things you may not even have considered as options."

Jordan thought for a moment. "But, she didn't really agree to the deal."

"Right. But as he said, she didn't really decline it either. So once the straw was gold she was stuck. In business it is usually best to make sure that everything is clearly spelled out. Even in 'handshake deals' clarity it everybody's friend," the Middle-Aged Man said. "Let's take a look at the end. She was facing losing what was most precious to her. However, even in her darkest hour, there was hope. She just had to do the impossible. Guess the name of a strange man who could spin straw into gold."

"I think she went about trying to solve the problem the right way. She asked advisors. She consulted resources. Her plan should have worked!" Jordan said.

"But, it didn't work. Did it?" the Middle-Aged Man replied. "Sometimes things we think should work, don't. You may have faced that at some point. Most people have. You think the plan or the response was perfect, but it fails. Why? Because we don't always see all the moving parts, the variables, if you will, of every problem. Often it is because we are standing too close to see clearly."

Jordan smiled. "That makes sense to me. I am so close to my situation and I have made it so personal, that I can't see the moving parts, the variables, very clearly at all. I can see the bad ending of this problem but no real solution. Maybe what I need is a better perspective of the situation."

"That is often true. Perhaps if you gain a different perspective, tomorrow morning will bring a solution you have not previously considered. I hope so. For all of our sakes," the Middle Aged-Man said.

Lessons IV

Jordan thanked the man and headed back to the top of the Big Tower. To the Big Office with the Big Desk to sit in the Big Chair. There was no doubt that Jordan was not certain how to proceed. As had happened in the past, Jordan decided to review the notes and see what significant things would jump out.

The first thing to jump out at Jordan in the review dealt with looking back. "It is easier to avoid problems than correct them." Jordan wrote:

Speak up honestly about the situation and sometimes you can avoid problems in the first place.

It seems that in the case of the Rumpelstiltskin story, things went from bad to worse when the future queen failed to speak up about what was going on. Jordan saw a real similarity in the merger problem. In the early days of the merger talks, if anyone saw a problem they certainly didn't say anything. Now they were in trouble that may have been avoidable.

As Jordan reflected on the first spinning of the straw into gold, it was obvious that Rumpelstiltskin took advantage of the situation and sought only his own profit. "That is a lot like what NIGHT did to FABLE. They saw a chance to help themselves at our expense and they moved right in. We just saw a chance to get out of what may have been a short term bad situation." Jordan wrote:

People of low character don't have your best interest in mind.

When you deal with others honestly and fairly, it is easier to be fooled by people who do not. Because the future queen was kind-hearted and tried to think the best of others, she became easy prey for Rumpelstiltskin who was neither of those things. On the second night of straw spinning, Rumpelstiltskin named an unreasonable price and the future queen was so shocked that she didn't respond. He took that as agreement while she was shocked that he thought they had made a deal. Again, her failure to speak up led to an even bigger problem. Jordan wrote:

In a negotiation no one will look after your interests as well as you so look after your interests.

Finally, Jordan reflected on the end of the story. The queen was in danger of losing her child, and she turned to what she thought were the best resources. When books and experts failed to deliver the correct answer, she was at a loss as to how to proceed. Ultimately, she decided to come forward and speak honestly with the king and ultimately to ask for help from the citizens of the kingdom. Almost too late she decided to speak up about the desperate situation in which she was now trapped. By turning to help from the kingdom as a whole she was able to find the answer to her riddle. Jordan wrote:

The wisdom of everybody together is often greater than the wisdom of anybody alone.

That was followed very quickly by the thought:

People who are overconfident are often surprised by how things turn out.

Jordan closed the notebook, turned off the light in the Big Office and went home. Tomorrow was a new day and perhaps a new perspective. Hopefully that perspective would provide the right answer.

The following day Jordan arrived early at FABLE. Calling a FABLE-wide meeting first thing in the morning, Jordan was both energized and embarrassed to address the employees. As the crowd gathered most were expecting bad news. Jordan delivered some.

"I am embarrassed to stand here in front of you and tell you that I have led FABLE into an agreement to merge with NIGHT. Now we are in danger of losing all that we as FABLE stand for. I take full RESPONSIBILITY. I tried to solve this problem myself. I couldn't. I consulted the Leadership Team. They couldn't. Now I turn to you. Each of you. Someone told me yesterday that the wisdom of everybody together is often greater than the wisdom of anybody alone. I am counting on that to be true."

"There is an out-clause to the merger agreement. We have six months to raise annual profits 19%. The efforts of each of us will be vital to make this happen. I need each of you to think about how you can help, just a little but maybe a lot, to reach that goal. Talk with your colleagues and your friends in the company. You can all reach me on the magic box. No idea is off the table but this: We don't change who FABLE is as a company or forget what is important to us."

The buzz in the room was audible and rising. The people who made up FABLE broke off into small groups or working alone started looking things up on their own portable magic box. That afternoon ideas began to come in. Some good. Some great. Some unworkable. But, each was assessed and considered. Everyone who sent in an idea received a personal response from Jordan, often asking for additional details, and often in person. The energy in Fable was at an all- time high. Jordan realized one additional point:

Workers value the company when the company values their work.

At the end of the six months many of the new ideas were in place. Some were still being implemented as other ideas continued to be proposed. Jordan pushed some form of the EQUALS key and discovered that profits were not up 19%. They were up 21%!

Of course, the people at NIGHT were shocked and enraged. At the end of the meeting Jordan said, "Guards, please escort these people from FABLE Tower."

The NIGHT team exited, and Jordan was left to attend the celebration with the employees who had worked so hard to save the company.

Problem Five

The problem with saving the company was people became very nervous about who would protect the company the next time it needed saving. The Big Bad Wolf, who people feared would show up soon, was never going to announce its arrival in advance.

Jordan enjoyed several productive years at FABLE after the merger was called off. However, now that the BBW that was NIGHT was no longer a problem, there was a problem that was Jordan's alone.

It wasn't an issue that appeared in the Big Tower, but it was an issue for the person who sat in the Big Chair in the Big Office. Jordan's spouse said, "It is time to retire and spend time with me and the family. You have dedicated your career to FABLE and we are grateful, but we want to see you more and do the things we have always put off until later."

Jordan was certainly interested in the idea of retirement. The idea of spending time doing…whatever.

But, the reality of not being in charge and not being at the top of FABLE Tower every day was more daunting than Jordan had first realized. It took a while to come to grips with the prospect, but eventually the thought of time with family became an actual list of things that would happen once Jordan turned off the lights for the last time in the Big Office at the top of the Big Tower. That list became things that Jordan began to desperately want to do.

"I am fortunate that I have built a brick house of a relationship with my spouse," Jordan thought. "However, to maintain that relationship now for the rest of my life, I need to realize that I have built something here that I can turn over to the next person so that I can do what only I can do. Namely be a spouse, a parent, a grandparent to my family."

So it was that Jordan drafted a lovely letter to the Board that was some form of THANKS for the opportunity to work for their entire career at FABLE. However, there were other things that now needed to take precedence while Jordan's health was still good, etc. Jordan signed the letter and carried it by hand to the Chair of the Board.

There was a hastily called Board meeting several days later. The Board, after much consideration, replied with some form of NO. Their reasons were good, if selfish.

"Only Jordan can make sure that FABLLE continues to be successful and protected from whatever BBWs might come to the neighborhood. While we understand the desire to retire, we believe a new compensation plan including some additional time off will allow Jordan to be with the family while still making sure that FABLE is in good hands. Jordan's hands," the Chair said.

While surprised that they had not agreed, secretly Jordan was some form of FLATTERED that the Board thought only one person could steer FABLE and Jordan was that person. Jordan's spouse was less enthused, but reluctantly agreed. Jordan initially took a bit more time off, enjoyed the extra money which was spent on the family, but eventually after a few years was in the Big Chair behind the Big Desk in the Big Office at the top of the Big FABLE Tower as much as before.

Jordan's spouse again made the request and Jordan again realized it was time to go. The Board again declined the resignation, and Jordan's loyalty to FABLE caused another six months to pass. Ultimately, Jordan knew that it was time to go, but knew as well that he did not know how to say goodbye in a way that would resonate with the Board. So, one morning he decided to try to get some good advice.

Walking down a floor to the door previously marked INFORMATION resulted in an awkward meeting with a newer executive who, while pleasant, was not who Jordan was looking for. Ultimately Jordan walked the entire building and ended up in the basement by the boiler.

There, on the original door from so many years ago, Jordan saw the sign marked INFORMATION.

Jordan smiled and knocked on the door. When there was no answer, Jordan knocked again with rhythm. Still there was no answer. With increasing desperation Jordan knocked a third time. Finally, the door swung open and there sat an Older Woman behind a battered desk.

"Good to see you could still find your way all the way down here Jordan," the Older Woman said. "What brings you down from the top of the tower?"

"I have a problem. It actually sounds silly when I say it out loud, but everyone seems to think I am indispensable to FABLE and I have almost begun to think so myself. I can't seem to figure out how to leave. I feel trapped. I love it here and I love the people here, but there are things I need to do. Why can't I go?"

The Older Woman thought for a while. "That is a problem, certainly not silly, and maybe not even that unusual. Are you sure you are ready to go?"

Jordan looked determined. "I am ready. It is hard to imagine leaving, but there are other things that I need to do. Can you tell me how to leave?"

The Older Woman smiled. "Now you know that it's not that simple. But guess what, I have a story I can share. Do you remember the story of Rapunzel?"

Rapunzel

Once upon a time a couple fell in love and got married. As often happens in these cases, the couple moved into a house on the edge of town and soon the wife was pregnant. Things were progressing normally when the young wife began to experience a series of food cravings. Some things were easy to find, pickles for example. During this time of history there was no ice cream so that was not an issue. But, the wife developed a craving for fresh peaches.

This was a problem because the only fresh peaches were on the tree of the scary property next door which was surrounded by a high fence. Finally, to ease his young wife's suffering, the young husband scaled the wall and took some of the peaches. He had almost made his escape when he felt a bony, but strong, hand grab his shoulder and something sharp touch his ribs. "Don't move or it will be the last thing you do," a cold voice said. "Why are you trespassing on my property and stealing my food?"

"Oh, in truth it is because I am desperate. My wife is pregnant, you see, and the only thing she can think of is peaches. You have the only ones in the area. I am desperate to help her," the man pleaded.

"Well enough," the voice said. "I will let you leave with the peaches you desperately want. But, I must have what I want as well."

In his desperation and without thinking, the man said, "I agree! Name your price and let me help my wife."

After a pause the voice said, "My price is the child. I want the baby when it is born. I will come around the day the baby is born and collect your payment."

The man was mortified. He heard a rustling sound behind him and when he turned he found he was standing alone in the orchard. "Surely in my fear I must have imagined the whole thing" he thought. "Who could take a child as payment for peaches?"

The man climbed the wall and presented the young wife with the peaches. In time he forgot the entire incident. But on the day his daughter was born, a woman with a cold voice showed up and demanded the child.

"Certainly, you are joking!" the man said.

The woman reminded him of the conversation and the promise he made that night in the orchard. The man knew he would have to give up his daughter or face death for thievery as it was a harsh land with harsh laws. So, telling his wife that they must surrender the baby, he took his daughter and placed her in the hands of the woman.

The woman took the girl and named her Rapunzel. The child and the woman moved away one night and were not seen again in those parts.

When Rapunzel was thirteen she threatened to run away, as teenagers sometimes do, from the woman she knew as her mother. So, the woman locked her in a tower with no door and just a single window. There the woman would visit every day to bring food. Rapunzel's hair was magically long, and she would lower the hair out the window and the pull the woman up as she held on to the hair.

When Rapunzel was older, a prince rode by and saw the woman entering the tower via Rapunzel's hair; he was immediately smitten with the woman Rapunzel had become. Once the older woman left the tower and went away, he called up to Rapunzel having heard the woman use her name. Rapunzel was smitten. He asked her to lower her hair, which she gladly did. The night passed with the two making plans to run away together. The prince left in the morning promising to return that evening.

Rapunzel attempted to reason with the woman when she returned that day. "You shall never leave me!" the woman said. "All I have ever wanted was someone to love. You are mine and will always be mine. Safe and secure in this tower where you are loved."

But Rapunzel did not feel loved. She felt trapped. When the Prince returned that evening she gladly let down her hair. The prince had devised a plan to cut her hair and tie it inside the room allowing them both to escape. The plan went surprisingly well. The woman did not return in the middle of the attempt. The hair didn't break. No one fell. No injuries. The two mounted the prince's horse and rode off to the prince's kingdom to live happily ever after.

The End

Aftermath V

"Well," Jordan said. "That one ended with more of an up note than most of the stories I have heard over the years."

The Older Woman smiled. "Not every story has a bad ending. Sometimes it is up to us to determine how things will end up. So, do you not like happy endings as a rule?"

"Not at all. I like happy endings as well as the next person. It's just not the type of story, or ending, I expected when I came in. But with that said, can we walk through the story? I don't want to get caught up on the ending alone and miss out on some of the other lessons to be learned from it" Jordan said.

"Certainly," said the Older Woman. "Let's start at the beginning and see what we can see. The story begins as most stories of this type do. Everything is great. The couple is in love. They get married. They are going to have a baby. Good times. That is how many of us look back and choose to see the beginning of our own story. True for you, or not?"

Jordan thought for a bit. "It is how I generally remember the beginning of my story as an adult. I came to work at FABLE and think of those years as going really well. But if I am honest with myself the first part of the story of my time here at FABLE was almost a nightmare. I had to decide to really buckle down and put in work like the third Little Pig in order to save my job and my career. But now when I look back, the work and the scare of maybe losing my job is just a distant memory and one that seems almost like it happened to someone else. I have kind of glossed over the 'near miss' of the actual events."

"I see. I think that is true of most of us. We tend to look back on the events of our life from a long time before and romanticize them. Sometimes making them better, sometimes worse, than they really were," the Older Woman said. "So, let's move on and look at the what causes the first major problem in the story. The young couple gets in a bind, like most young couples do, and they end up solving a short-term problem with a long-term solution. That long-term solution often extracts a steep price. Looking back, we can see the difference. But in the moment, without the advantage of some form of WISDOM, we often make poor decisions."

"Right! Now I wonder why they didn't attempt to buy the peaches up front or negotiate price they could pay? It almost seems silly," Jordan said.

"To someone with WISDOM, people making foolish choices always seems silly. But, how do we gain wisdom? By making foolish choices. Then paying a steep price. And finally, if we pay attention, figuring out what we did wrong and what we should have done instead so we don't pay the price a second time," the Older Woman said.

"That makes sense," Jordan began. "But, once the woman took the baby why did she lock her in a tower?"

"The same reason the biological parents made the trade for the peaches and no police. She simply wanted what she wanted. She wanted it now and didn't care about the price or the consequences. You can surely see some alternatives to locking your child in a tower with no door?" the Older Woman asked.

Jordan laughed. "Of course. That was always going to end poorly. The one thing the woman wanted was to have companionship. By locking Rapunzel in the tower she ensured that the girl was not with her all day which denied her the companionship she wanted short-term. And it almost guaranteed Rapunzel would leave as soon as possible which denied her companionship long-term. Silly. No one will consent to being locked up forever if they can help it."

"Exactly right! That is WISDOM speaking right there. What about the end? A Prince showed up and together they executed an escape. How did they pull that off?" The Older Woman asked. "They used things that were always there that were overlooked by Rapunzel and the woman. But when the prince wanted to get her out of the tower because he loved her, the solution seemed simple. Because it was. She always had her hair and there was always furniture in the room she lived in. Simple."

Jordan thought for a bit. "It does seem simple. All you have to do is stop and think. Think about what you know, what you want, and what you have at hand. Then put it all together and do what is best for you and the people important to you."

Jordan smiled and jumped up. "Of course! I have to go but thank you! Again. As always, you have pointed me in the right direction! I want to get moving that way while the path is clear in my mind."

As Jordan reached the door the Older Woman said, "Jordan. The path was always right there in front of you. If you go down that path, I am sure you will find the happy ending you are looking for."

Lessons V

Jordan thanked the woman and headed back to the office. Flipping through the notes in the tattered 30 plus year old notebook, Jordan was excited about the future. For a while it seemed that being the Leader of FABLE was what was in store for a large portion of the remainder of Jordan's life. Yet, much like Rapunzel, Jordan felt trapped by something that wanted to believe it had Jordan's best interest at heart. But, that wasn't true.

As Jordan reflected on the story of Rapunzel the first thing that jumped out were the mistakes the parents made. Jordan wrote:

Short-term problems only deserve short-term solutions.

Making a long-term commitment to solve the need of the moment put them in a huge mess. They lost their child in that case, but Jordan knew of others who had applied long-term solutions to short-term problems. They lacked WISDOM. It seemed only by looking back could you really grow and know what to do. Jordan wrote:

Wisdom is expensive so use the Wisdom you buy.

It seemed like most people were just not willing to take the time to think things through. Jordan made a promise to himself that going forward the WISDOM purchased by mistakes and hard times would be spent on avoiding future situations that caused pain and needless expense. Jordan thought of the woman who took the baby because she wanted companionship, yet her single-minded desire to hold on to the one thing she valued most led her to lose that very thing. It seemed obvious locking Rapunzel in the tower would end badly, and it did. For the woman. As Rapunzel and the Prince rode away there was no mention of goodbye or even a backwards glance. The woman ended up living her worst fear, being truly alone. Jordan wrote:

Not all decisions are ours to make.

Jordan realized that certain decisions would always be made by others, but we cannot dictate everything to make the world fit our plans and schemes. It was fine to try to anticipate what others might do, but it was foolish to think that others were not working towards their own preferences and plans while we were working on our own.

One of the things that really struck Jordan in the notes was that Rapunzel had the means to escape the whole time. Yes, the Prince showed her the way, but the Prince didn't bring the means of escape. Those Rapunzel always had with her. She stayed in the tower because she couldn't imagine leaving the tower. Once the Prince arrived she could imagine a different life and without a backwards glance she left. Jordan wrote:

We can't blame others for being in a cage we helped build nor can others blame us when we choose to leave.

Jordan closed the notebook. The WISDOM gained from a long and successful career lay between the covers of the notebook. Smiling, Jordan thought back on what had been learned. Many of the lessons Jordan wished had been learned earlier. But, what was obvious was that WISDOM was expensive and the result of mistakes and pain. Perhaps looking at the mistakes of others would be enough for some to learn, but Jordan often had to make the mistakes himself and feel the pain personally. Now with the WISDOM of a career to draw on Jordan knew what was going to happen next.

Jordan wrote a brief note and left it on the desk. Jordan got up from the Big Chair, from behind the Big Desk, in the Big Office, at the top of the Big Tower. A picture of Jordan's spouse caught his eye. Smiling, Jordan picked up the photo and, turning off the light, walked out of the Big Office for the last time without a backwards glance.

Ending

Jordan left that night and did not return to FABLE. Much-deserved time with the family awaited, and Jordan was not going to wait even a minute longer to begin the next phase of life. When Jordan's Administrative Assistant arrived the next morning, he was surprised to find that Jordan was not yet in. Checking the office, he found the note Jordan had left:

I am leaving Charlie in charge. I have

cut my hair and gone out to pursue my

Happily Ever After.

Jordan

The Assistant was floored. Charlie was frightened. But in the end, everything went fine. Were there bumps on the road? Certainly. But, there had been bumps before Jordan left. You see, Jordan discovered the WISDOM to know that everyone was replaceable in a company, but no one could replace you in your family.

While on a nice vacation in a nice country on a nice beach, Jordan wrote to Charlie.

"I know my leaving seemed sudden to you, and it was. But, you were ready. My being there any longer was holding you back. In the back of the bottom file drawer in the Big desk you will find an old notebook with some things I learned over the course of my time at FABLE. Look it over if you have time. Perhaps you will learn from my mistakes and not feel obligated to make some of them yourself. If you ever get stuck and think there isn't a way out, think about some of the old stories you know but may have forgotten. When I took the time to remember, I realized that I always knew the answer."

The End.

Thank You's

FABLE would not have come together in my mind or in print if not for the understanding of my FAMILY and the help of my FRIENDS. To my wife Jackie: Thank you for being supportive through our many years as I chased my career in its many forms. I always know you love me. To my kids Kelsy & Slade; Thank you for understanding when I was out helping others and you wished I was home with you. I know you have taught me more than I have taught you. To my brother Kemo: Thank you for refusing to hear this story and telling me to write it down instead. That is good advice to anyone who wants to be a writer. To my friend Jim: Thank you for listening to me and editing FABLE. You have always been my friend. To my students both current and former: Thank you for being willing to listen to my stories. You know that I was always trying to impart some form of WISDOM you could use when I was gone. Finally, to the readers of FABLE: Take the time to think about what you know and the path will usually become clear. If not, there is no shame in asking someone for a hand, or a story.

Dr. Long is the Chair of Doctoral Studies at William Woods University in Fulton, Missouri. He is a retired superintendent, principal, and teacher. A consummate storyteller he is available to speak to your organization, be it school or business, about how to use stories to improve our lives and companies. He can be reached at: FABLEwisdom@gmail.com

Made in the USA
Middletown, DE
09 February 2019